Why The Moon Moves Away

by Bradley James Weber
illustrated Ryan Pentney

raintree

a Capstone company — publishers for children

Engage Literacy is published in the UK by Raintree.
Raintree is an imprint of Capstone Global Library Limited, a company incorporated in England and Wales having its registered office at 264 Banbury Road, Oxford, OX2 7DY – Registered company number: 6695582

www.raintree.co.uk

© 2018 by Raintree. All rights reserved. No part of this publication may be reproduced, stored in a retrieval system, or transmitted in any way or by any means, electronic, mechanical, photocopying, recording or otherwise, without the prior written permission of Capstone Global Library Limited.

Editorial credits
Karen Soll, editor; Cynthia Della-Rovere, designer; Steve Walker, production specialist

21 20 19 18 17
10 9 8 7 6 5 4 3 2 1
Printed and bound in India.

Why the Moon Moves Away

ISBN: 978 1 4747 4633 5

Contents

CHAPTER 1
CRACK THIS THING OPEN.............4

CHAPTER 2
HOW ABOUT A SWAP? 16

CHAPTER 3
BEYOND TASTE,
BEYOND EXPLANATION 26

CHAPTER 4
THE BATTERED SHORE 34

CHAPTER 5
IN UP TO THE SHOULDER 44

CHAPTER 6
STAY OUT OF THEIR WAY............50

CHAPTER 7
BEAUTIFUL BECAUSE OF THEM 58

THE SCIENCE BEHIND THE STORY 64

Chapter 1
Crack this thing open

Long ago, back in the days when the world was new and people had yet to walk upon it, Earth had no Moon. The Sun was there, as it always had been, giving light and warmth to everything it touched. But it rose and set alone.

In that same long ago, back in the days before the Moon circled the world, there lived a Raven. Even then Raven was a scavenger living on whatever she could find. It was usually the scraps and rubbish left behind by bigger animals such as Bear, Jaguar, Wolf and Lion. Because they ate often, they were very messy and left their meals unfinished.
This worked out well for Raven.

But one morning was different. Not a bite could be found.

She looked in all the usual places, then in all the *un*-usual places. Then she really started searching.

All day long she searched the forest for hidden berries, overripe fruit and spoiled vegetables. She scanned the beach for dead fish or maybe, hopefully, some tasty little crabs.

She found exactly nothing to eat – no insect, no spider, not even a worm.

Accepting her hunger, Raven rode a lazy breeze along the beach. She had just turned towards home when she spied movement on the sand. After looping around, she landed behind the wiggling lump where she could study it from safety.

Longer than it was tall and round on every side, Raven guessed the faded brown thing was a piece of driftwood. Based on its size, she suspected it hid at least a few crabs. Just the thought of them made her even hungrier.

The lump had been still since she landed, so she inched over and poked it with her beak. No crabs ran out, so she hit it again. Every time she hit it, it made a solid *tok* and rocked back and forth. After a few more pokes, this became a game.

Forgetting how hungry she was, Raven jabbed it again and again, making the thing wobble deeper and faster. Then it rolled all the way over, revealing the face of her worst enemy in the world.

"Rat! I should've known!"

7

Like Raven, Rat was a scavenger. This made them terrible enemies that waged a war over food. Whenever they found the same leftovers, they never failed to start a fresh round of screeching, shouting and carrying on. And one of them always went away full of bad feelings and an empty stomach.

The word for this kind of angry, unfriendly behaviour is "hostility".

Rat's *hostility* towards Raven was huge and severe.

Raven was *hostile* towards Rat and getting more so by the second.

She beat her wings and called him all the usual names, including ones she knew would drive him away from whatever he had been pecking at.

It had to be food. Rat didn't hunt for anything less. True, he had been crawling inside of it, which was disgusting, but Raven would worry about that later.

Rat stayed totally still, totally calm, and said nothing. When he had heard enough of Raven's noise, he asked, "Are you hungry? You can have some of this when you've finished screeching."

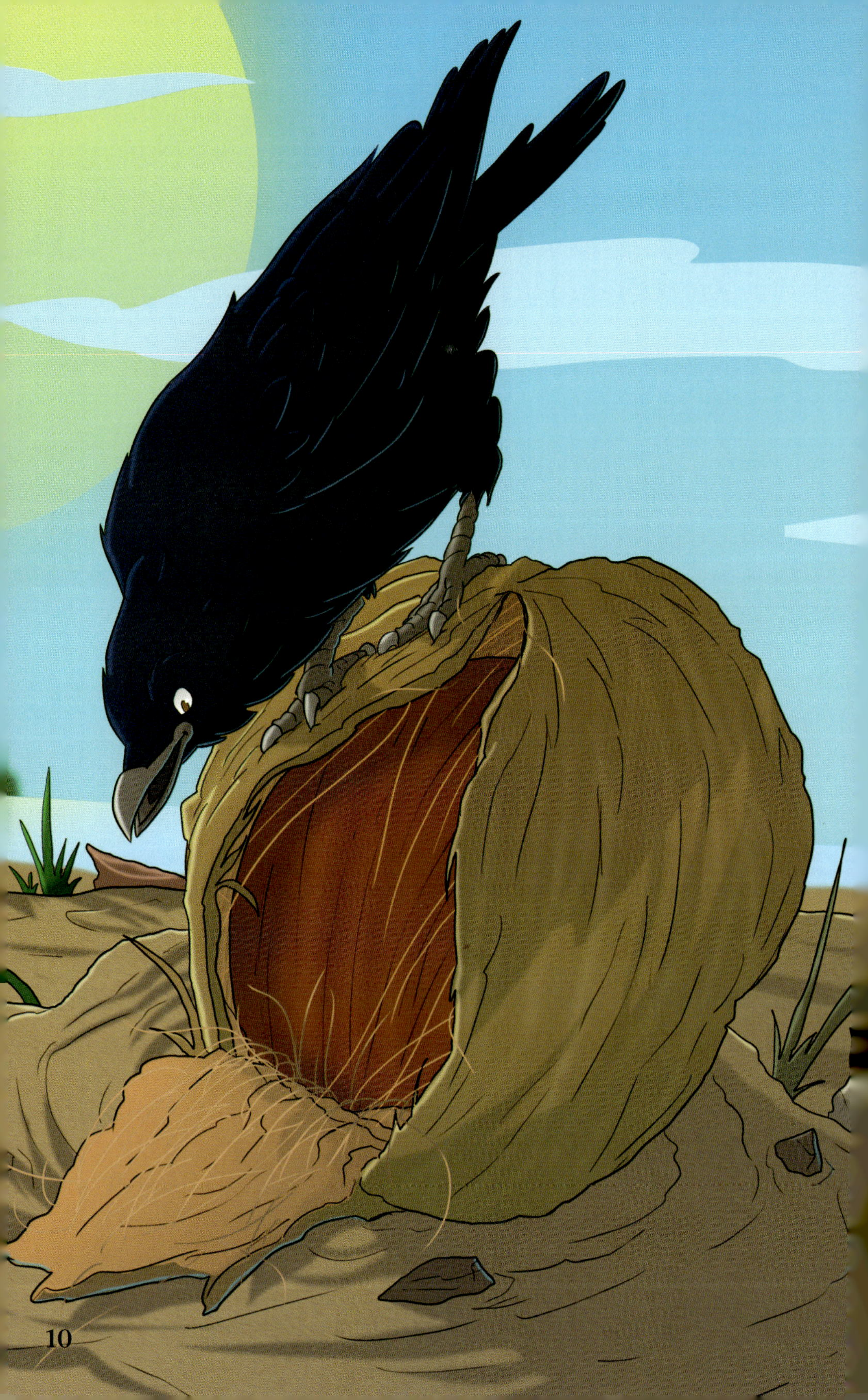

Raven looked at Rat who said, "Great idea. There's plenty here, and I can't eat it all. Honestly, I'm tired of fighting with you. It doesn't do us any good."

Raven stared at his little rat face, trying to decode what dirty rat tricks he was up to. Finally, she decided he really was offering her both something to eat and an end to their constant battles.

Raven asked, "Are you offering to share? Why? We hate each other! I mean, I thought we did. Don't we?"

"I don't hate you. We fight over food, that's all. I've worked out where to find plenty of it, more than I can eat actually, but getting at it is a serious issue. If we solve that problem, we can stop scavenging and eating everybody else's rubbish. Good plan, don't you think? All we need to do is crack this thing open."

Raven gave the thing a long look. What she had mistaken for driftwood was a broken husk with an inside full of tough, brown fibres like dry grass.

She couldn't eat that, but the seed at the bottom of the husk had promise. It was the size and shape of a grapefruit, dark brown and covered with the same rough fibre that filled the husk.

Rat told her that the seed was where the good stuff was.

"So you've had one," said Raven. "How did you open it?"

"I pushed it off a cliff onto some rocks, but I'm convinced there's a better way to open it."

"Fine," Raven sighed. "What can I do?"

Rat told her to use her beak to break the shell. Raven pecked it without effect. She pecked harder and harder, hammering it until her beak ached and her head rang, but she couldn't make a crack.

"Ridiculous," she huffed. "What do you call this thing, anyway?"

Rat said he thought it might be a coconut.

Raven grumbled that whatever it was, there had to be a way into it.

While she waited for her sore beak to stop throbbing and her pained head to clear, Rat told her about the coconut and the cliff. He described his method for cracking his first coconut.

Then he asked, "Could you fly it up there? The coconut to the cliff."

Raven's brain worked out Rat's plan. She would haul the coconut to the cliff and push it off to break the shell.

She considered the coconut's weight and eyed the distance to the cliff. Then she said, "Let's find out."

With nothing to lose, they tore the fibres from around the coconut until it toppled out of the husk. Raven pounced on it, dug in her claws and beat her wings with everything she had. Finally, with some help from that lazy sea breeze, she and the coconut were airborne.

Raven heard Rat's cheers as she sailed over shrubs, between branches, then through the tops of the tallest trees. Battling to climb up into the sky, she rose towards the cliff then felt the coconut slip from her grasp.

"No!" she cried. She whipped around in time to see the coconut bounce off the rocks and into the bush.

Even before she landed, Raven began to apologize. "I'm so sorry, Rat! I really thought I had it."

"Sorry for what? That was perfect."

Before them lay the broken coconut. Its bright white meat was just waiting to be eaten.

Chapter 2
How about a swap?

Before too long, Rat and Raven perfected a system for breaking open coconuts. Not only did they enjoy the tasty white part, but they also discovered the coconut water was more delicious than the meat.

Even so, they were getting tired of eating coconuts day after day. Yes, they ate berries and bugs and fruit and crabs whenever those could be found, but most of their meals consisted of coconuts.

Sometimes one of them would hint at going back to dining on leftovers. Not full time, of course, but just for a change. Then the other would remind the one of their plan to stop scavenging, so they'd crack open another coconut.

One day, while picking fibres from around what seemed like their thousandth coconut, who should wander by but Bear, carrying a big chunk of dinner.

Bear had fur the same faded brown as a coconut husk, and he seemed enormous as he towered over the animals. He was also unbelievably strong. He was tougher than Rhino, meaner than Badger, lazier than Jaguar and smarter than Ox, but not by much. Bear could also flex his muscles when he wanted to, which was usually when wrestling his best friend, Crocodile.

Every once in a while a creature who is tough and mean and fast and strong starts to believe it can do whatever it wants and whenever it wants. Bear felt this way all the time, which allowed him to snatch the coconut without asking for permission or saying, "Hello".

Gripping his warm dinner in one paw, Bear held the rough, brown seed in his other. He brought it to his eye, shook it by his ear, heard a slosh and demanded to know what it was.

Rat replied, "Good morning, Bear. Long time, no see. How've you been?"

Bear huffed through his nose. "What is this thing?"

Rat declared it was a one-hundred-percent pure, wild-caught coconut. He watched Bear sniff it twice more before saying, "You eat it."

"I know you eat it," lied Bear. "What does it taste like?"

Rat's brain fought to recall what, if anything, he had eaten that tasted the least bit like coconut. It was useless. The only thing that tasted like coconut was coconut.

Bear began to snarl as he waited for an answer.

Rat looked to Raven for help. She, too, charged through memories only to come up with the exact same answer as Rat.

"It tastes like coconut."

The coconut thumped to the ground.

Bear said, "That was funny. Do you know how funny you are?"

His eyes narrowed and his tongue passed over his lip with a hearty *smack*.

"Do you know what else? I like funny birds."

Rat tried to squeeze between Bear and his friend in order to separate them.

"You've never had a coconut before, have you? How about a swap? We give you this one, and you give us some of your tasty . . . whatever that is. We'll even break it open for you. That's a deal-and-a-half, my friend. What do you say?"

They watched Bear puzzle over this for a while. Finally, he asked, "Don't you two usually fight over who is going to eat my leftovers?"

Raven told him that was a long time ago.

He laughed at her and replied, "Not that long ago."

After giving it further thought, Bear agreed to try their little snack then flopped under a low tree while they got cracking. Rat and Raven delivered the pieces in no time, but they found Bear already asleep in the shade.

They argued in whispers. Rat wanted to take the part of the dinner Bear owed them, but Raven convinced him otherwise. What if Bear would have given them more than they would have taken? Or worse, what if they ate too much and made him angry? Fearing to make either mistake, they busied themselves until evening, listening to Bear snore and their stomachs complain.

As soon as the Sun set, Bear's eyes opened to the coconut. He sneered, "It took you long enough," scraped the white stuff into his mouth and swallowed without bothering to chew.

"Not bad," he yawned. "Let me know when you've got more."

Then he picked up his dinner and headed towards the forest.

Rat called, "Hey, wait! What about our deal?"

Bear dropped his dinner. He sulked back to pick up the empty coconut shells, doubled-up his paw and *squeeeeezed* until the shells stopped breaking. Then he blew the dust at Rat and Raven.

"Next time," coughed Rat. "No rush."

Bear grabbed his dinner and disappeared into the forest.

"Robbed! Duped! Flimflammed!"

Raven had no idea what Rat was saying, but she knew he was fuming.

In all the time they had been enemies, she had never seen him like this.

"Bilked! Swindled! Scammed!"

Clearly, Rat had something on his mind. On and on he went shouting, stomping around, gnashing his teeth and growling.

When Raven had heard enough of Rat's noise she asked, "Do all those fancy words mean that we were tricked?"

"Exactly!" howled Rat. "That no-good . . . *bear* . . . is a . . . *thief*! He *tricked* us out of dinner, *stole* our coconut and *now* I'm *hungrier* than *ever*!"

Raven said, "We've been tricked. So what?"

Lying on the ground to catch his breath, Rat told Raven that she seemed to be taking it quite well.

Raven said, "Perhaps I hide my anger better than you do."

Rat thought about their many battles and suggested that she guess again.

"Or maybe," she said, "I know that we'll never starve."

Rat scrunched his face into a pout. "Because we'll always have coconuts?"

"Exactly," laughed Raven. "Because we'll always have coconuts."

Chapter 3
Beyond taste, beyond explanation

    Days came, days went, and Rat and Raven ate whatever fresh food they found. This was mostly coconuts. While they felt much better than they had when eating everybody's rotting leftovers, they stayed on the lookout for a variety of foods to balance their menu.

    As for swapping coconuts, Rat knew the idea remained sound. Sure, Bear had cheated them, but Rat believed others would treat them fairly. They just needed to be careful with whom they dealt.

One afternoon while searching the beach, they spied something in the surf, floating on its back while snacking on a crab.

Paddling towards the shallows, the stranger waved. Then he called, "Permission to come ashore?" to which Rat and Raven called, "Permission granted! Come on up!"

He was an odd creature with grey fur, stubby ears and a weathered, friendly face full of whiskers like the ones Walrus kept. Rat thought the stranger looked like a cross between a weasel and a wet cat, but he was nowhere near as mean as a wet cat.

"Ahoy, beachcombers," said the stranger. "Otter's the name, and who might you be?"

Before they knew it, the three of them spent the day on details that all new friends share. They talked about who they were, where they came from, what their families were like, things they did and things they ate. This last topic led to a long talk about all kinds of food. They discussed coconuts, something that Otter had never eaten, and crabs, which he ate often. But as much as he enjoyed crabs, he preferred one meal above all others.

"Crabs are sweet, to be sure. Sweeter still are those delicious little oysters."

"What are oysters?" asked Raven.

Otter thought about everything he had ever eaten, trying to remember if any of it tasted the least bit like oysters, but it was useless. What made oysters so delicious was beyond taste, beyond explanation.

When Otter understood that it was impossible to describe oysters to anyone who had never eaten one, he stopped trying. Instead, he told Rat and Raven to sit tight, and then he dove into the sea.

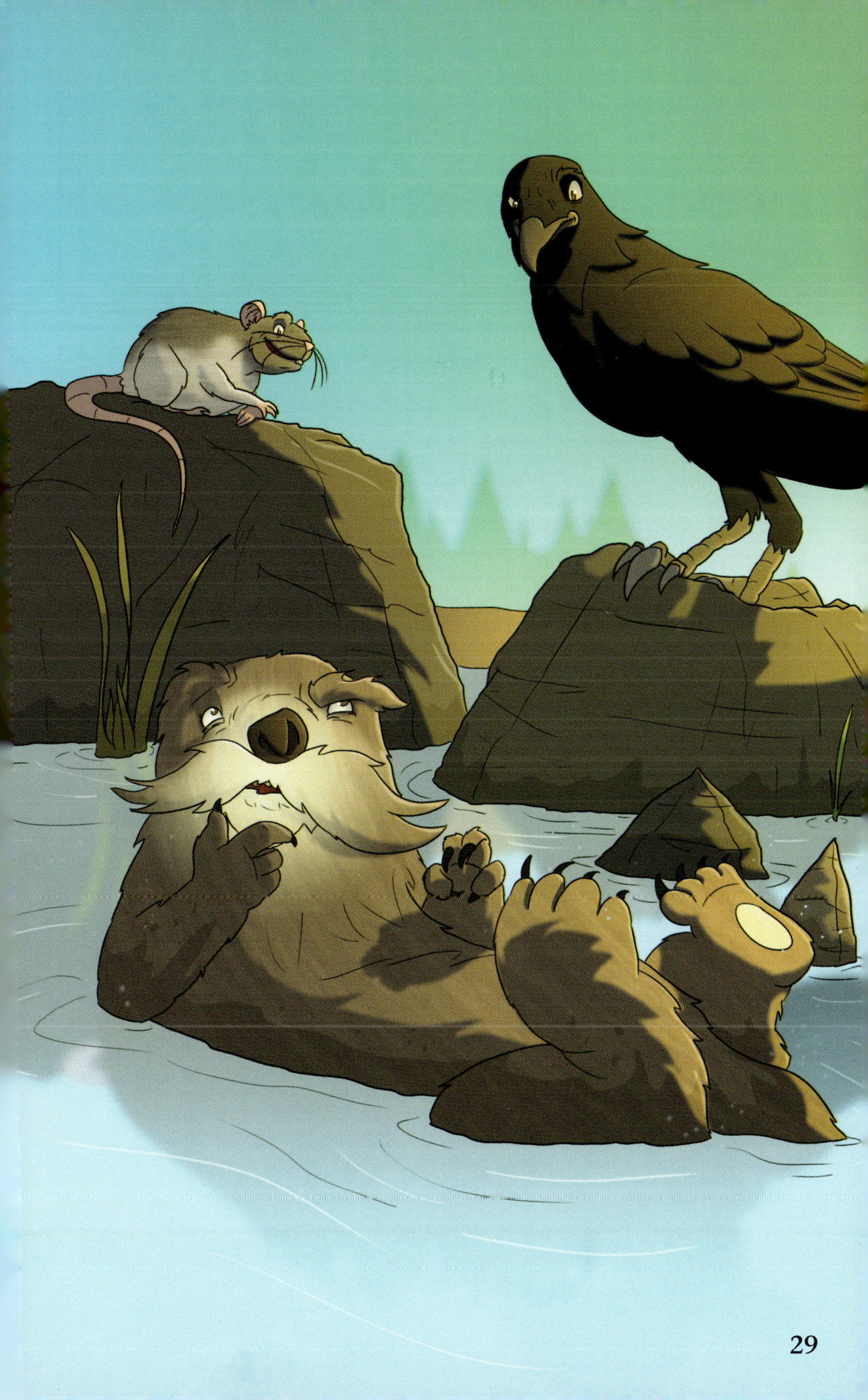

Rat and Raven saw him surface clutching two rocks, a lumpy grey one and one with a pointy top. Otter set the first rock on his stomach with the point facing skywards. He whacked the lumpy rock against it a few times, then he brought the lumpy rock ashore. He flicked away chunks and shards to get at the pale, creamy meat that he shared with his new friends.

They agreed it was one of the greatest things they'd ever tasted.

As well as the meat, Raven found that she loved looking at the gleaming white inside of the broken shell. Turning her head one way, the white inside had a golden shine. Turning her head another way, the shell flashed pink or green, or maybe a purplish-blue. She decided to take a piece of the shell back to her nest.

On the other half of the oyster Rat found a small, smooth stone the same gleaming white as the shell's inside.

Otter said it was a pearl. "They turn up sometimes. They're useless, but my grandchildren like them. They treat those trinkets like a prize."

Otter explained pearls came in different colours and sizes and warned them to be careful of getting them in their mouths.

"They're as hard as rocks, so don't try chewing them, just spit them out. Trust me – you don't want broken teeth or one of these stuck in your throat," said Otter.

Rat asked whether Otter wanted to try a coconut. If he liked it, they could set up a regular swap. Otter explained that while he didn't eat fruit or vegetables, he felt sure they could work out some sort of deal.

The new friends would have kept talking, but the old sea otter felt a change in the air. He scanned the sea's horizon and spied tremendous clouds looming across the water. Lightning slashed from the storm's dark edge and long, bright flashes ripped from the top.

Otter told Rat and Raven to find somewhere high and dry and out of the wind. Rat said he knew a mountain cave where they could lay low for a while.

"Good," said Otter. "Get going because we're in for some terrible weather."

Then he jumped in the sea and swam for home.

Chapter 4
The battered shore

Two days later, Rat and Raven dragged themselves from their hideout. They had done little more than wait out the storm, but they were exhausted. The weather had been so terrifying that neither had slept much. Now that the worst was over, they needed something to eat.

Rat picked his way down the slick rocks while Raven searched for food. After a long while, she brought him a smashed banana left by another animal and details of what she had seen. Everywhere lay broken branches. She found a valley filled by a mudslide and a raging river that had previously been a stream. Towards the beach lay a long, high wall of felled trees. How it happened or what it hid, she had no idea.

Rat guessed that a huge wave had crashed ashore, ripped everything out of the ground, and pushed it inland before it dragged the rest back out to sea. Just the thought of it made Raven sad. She hoped Otter was all right. When Rat told her that Otter was fine, she wanted to know how he knew.

"He's been through worse than a little wind and lightning. Trust me," Rat said to her. "Otter will show up sooner or later."

Rat finished eating then started down the cliff, a little faster than before. He really wanted to see that beach.

Whatever Rat's hopes had been for how the beach would look, the reality was far, far worse. Nearly all the sand had vanished, exposing a shelf of bare rocks. Some were so sharp and ugly that even the waves seemed afraid to roll over them. Washed ashore was all manner of storm debris – thick ropes of seaweed, the titanic jawbone of a long-dead sea monster and slime-covered boulders. There were also chunks of coral reef, thousands of dead fish and a huge blob of black gunk with shells stuck in it.

The battered shore was crowded with seagulls there to eat whatever could be eaten. Rat and Raven walked among the greedy birds, snacked on crabs and wandered the beach. They were amazed by how it had changed.

All morning animals came to survey the beach and eat what the sea had left behind. Everyone said it felt good to be out in the Sun, except for the seagulls. They were unhappy that they had to share the beach with others. The Sun tracked through the cloudless sky, rising higher, getting hotter and baking everything onto the rocks. Even so, the shore was more crowded than ever.

Rat and Raven talked about leaving but then spied Otter standing on a huge grey boulder thrown ashore by the storm. Glad to see him, Raven flew over to make sure Otter's family was all right and to keep him company while waiting for Rat to catch up. After the three friends finished sharing their storm stories, Raven pecked the thing they sat on. "Is this what I think it is?"

Otter nodded and grinned as he said, "Probably the biggest oyster there ever was."

Rat examined the shell's thick ridges. "How can we break into it?"

Otter took a pointy rock in both hands and whacked the oyster over and over without even chipping the shell.

"I knew that wouldn't work," he wheezed, "but it would have been foolish not to try."

Behind them, waves of angry gulls stirred then settled back to their feeding places. Between excited wings came flashes of fur the colour of coconut husks, a pair of yellow eyes and a dangerous tooth-filled mouth. Something big was coming their way.

39

"Well, well, well – if it isn't my old friend Rat and his funny bird friend. How's the coconut trade?"

"Nice to see you, Bear," said Rat, and he meant it. Bear could not have come at a better time. He was going to help them break into the oyster. He just didn't know it yet.

"Bear, this is Otter. Otter, meet Bear."

Otter gave a friendly nod. Bear ignored him and asked, "Do you know Crocodile?" as if they were already old friends.

Rat said, "Of course," even though they had done their best *not* to meet him.

Crocodile was as mean, fast, strong and lazy as Bear. Like Bear, he believed in doing whatever he wanted, whenever he wanted. What he wanted most was to be soaking in his lagoon, not standing around in the heat being nice to strangers. Saying nothing, he tried to cool off by breathing through his open mouth full of large and sharp teeth.

"Anyway," said Bear, "why are you pounding on the rock?"

This was exactly the question for which Rat had been waiting. "We'll tell you, but you have to help us open it and promise to share what's inside."

Raven turned to Rat, "Are you out of your mind? He . . . *swindled* us, remember?"

"I did not!" huffed Bear, who had no idea what the word meant.

Raven reminded Bear how he had eaten their coconut then walked off without sharing his dinner.

"You, sir," Raven hissed, "are a thief and a liar!"

"That's not true!" whined Bear. "Rat said I could pay up next time, but I forgot."

Before Raven had a chance to get really hostile, Rat dragged her behind the oyster.

"The only way we can do this is with help. Remember how we started with the coconuts? We worked together. Before that we spent all day fighting and starving."

Raven said he was being dramatic and was overreacting.

"Maybe. But we haven't gone hungry in I don't know how long. Even if we could crack it ourselves, this thing is huge! Either we share it, or it goes to waste. We'll tell them that we get a big chunk off the top, they get the rest, that way everybody goes home happy."

Raven felt like pouting, but a beak and feathers are useless for that kind of thing. Instead she warned Rat, "They're going to trick us."

Rat shrugged and said, "Even if they do, we'll never starve, and I think you know why."

She told him not to say it.

So he smiled at her and whispered, *"Because we'll always have coconuts."*

Chapter 5
In up to the shoulder

Bear's toes tapped on the rock he'd put by his feet. It was big and sharp and mean looking. Also, it was much heavier and harder than other rocks its size. Otter said that made it perfect for breaking into oysters.

Bear gave a yawn of boredom and watched Rat climb up the huge shell. Rat stood on the spot Otter said to strike with the rock and asked Bear if he was ready.

Bear snorted and said, "I'm ready."

"Right. Good. One more thing. Raven wants you to say it again."

"Seriously?"

"She's still upset about the coconut deal."

"Fine. Whatever it takes to get us closer to dinner."

Staring directly at Raven, Bear said, "I do hereby solemnly swear, *again*, to break open this oyster and share what's inside."

Clearly, Raven refused to believe Bear, but she nodded anyway.

Bear sneered and jerked his thumb at Rat to get off the oyster.

Rat jumped, barely hitting the ground before Bear heaved the rock and – *wham, wham, wham* – pounded it exactly where Rat had stood. The third strike went from a *crack* to a *crunch* that buried the rock in the shell's new hole.

Too stunned to even cheer at this enormous feat, the three friends watched Bear throw down the rock then flick away shards of shell.

Raven found herself saying, "That was amazing! Well done."

Rat and Otter said similar things that Bear pretended not to hear.

When the hole was big enough, Bear jammed his arm in up to the shoulder and hauled out a large chunk of meat. He took four mouth-filling bites then flung the rest at Crocodile.

"You're right," said Bear, already tearing out more of the oyster. "This is great!"

Crocodile grumped, "I've had better," and gobbled another piece.

When Raven screamed, "*What is wrong with you?*" even the seagulls took notice. "You promised! *Twice!* Remember?"

Bear smirked around another mouthful. "Yeah, I promised to share, but I didn't promise to share with *you*."

47

Powerless to stop them, the three friends watched Bear and Crocodile stuff themselves until the only thing left was a runny blob on Bear's brown fur. He threw it at their feet, said, "There's yours," and turned to walk away.

Trailing a little behind, Crocodile lashed his heavy tail against the empty oyster, hoping the noise would scare everybody. Instead, the top half of the shell flew into the water. Rocking in the shell's bottom half was the biggest, brightest, most beautiful pearl anyone had ever seen.

49

Chapter 6
Stay Out of Their Way

The pearl was bigger than the rock Bear had used on the oyster. It was bigger than his head. Rolling it between his paws, hints of gold flashed across the perfect whiteness.

"Pretty," he said and shook it by his ear. Hearing nothing he asked, "What is it?"

Otter told him exactly what he had told Rat and Raven. "Pearls are rubbish, and they can't be chewed. Make sure you spit them out to avoid breaking your teeth or getting one stuck in your throat."

Crocodile huffed, "Now who's the liar?"

Otter said he had no reason to lie.

"Really? You're not cross that we ate the whole oyster? You don't want to save this for yourselves?"

Then Crocodile said that pearls were probably the same as oysters and coconuts. To get at the good stuff, they had to be cracked open.

Bear turned to the three friends. "Tricking us out of dessert, eh? If you'd have shared, we might have saved you some."

51

Bear tried crushing the pearl in his paws, and then he tried clawing at it, but neither worked. Before Bear had a chance to smash it on a rock, Crocodile said he wanted a go. He grabbed the pearl with his front teeth, opened his mouth to the limit and caught the pearl in his back teeth. This is the strongest part of his jaw.

"What do we do?" asked Raven.

Otter said, "What *can* we do?"

"Nothing," sighed Rat, "except stay out of their way."

Crocodile's teeth closed on the pearl with all their power. He kept adding pressure, growling, straining, putting more force through his jaws than ever before. But the pearl refused to crack.

During a rest, he searched for the faintest seam, the tiniest hole in which to sink his teeth. He found nothing. The pearl was perfect.

So he chewed it, testing for hidden weakness. Every snap of those fierce jaws, every crunch of those terrible teeth gouged a series of dents in the gleaming white globe.

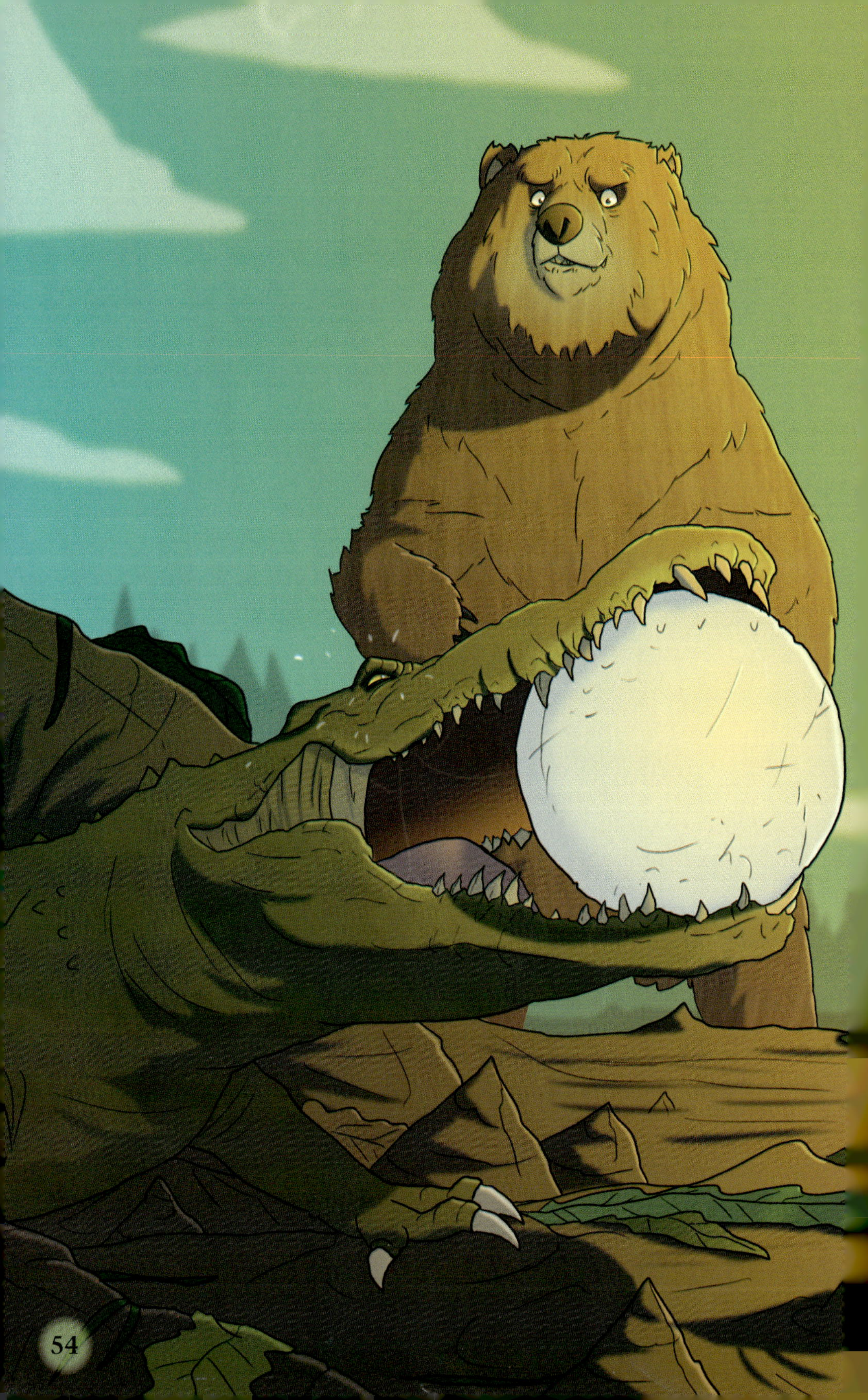

The ruin of its beauty broke Raven's heart.

"Stop!" she cried.

Crocodile gave the pearl another vicious chomp. Rat and Otter held her back from flying at Crocodile, but let her scream at the top of her lungs.

Bear had heard enough of Raven's noise. He said to Crocodile, "Let's go."

Crocodile mumbled something around the pearl.

"Fine. But it's your last chance."

Crocodile grinned. This was it. He could feel it. He rolled the battered pearl to his very back teeth. Ready for this final crushing bite, he took a deep breath and felt the pearl drop into his throat.

He tried to swallow then tried to cough. He tried to close his mouth then open it wider and tried to move the pearl in any direction, but it would not budge. He tried to plead for help, but he could not make a sound. He tried to breathe but got no air.

Blind panic took over Crocodile's massive body. Crocodile whipped his head and tail in every direction. He stomped, rolled around and did whatever he could to get rid of the pearl. None of it worked.

"He's choking!" shouted Otter. "Slap him on the back!"

Bear leapt on his flailing friend, pinned him to the ground and slammed the heel of his paw between Crocodile's shoulders. He did this, again and again, with no effect.

The pearl stayed stuck.

If he didn't get some air soon, Crocodile could die.

Otter shouted, "Get him up! Get him up off the ground! Good, now watch me."

With Rat's help, Otter showed Bear where to stand and where to wrap his arms around Crocodile's middle. Then Otter showed him how to grab one fist in the other and squeeze and pull them hard into his friend's stomach.

"Do it right above his belly. Make it quick, like you're trying to lift him. Now!"

Bear squeezed and heaved, squeezed and heaved, doing everything he could to save his friend's life.

On Bear's fourth squeeze, Crocodile let out a loud *pflunghk* and deep gulps of air filled his chest. Bear laid his gasping, wheezing friend on the shore, giving them both a chance to catch their breath.

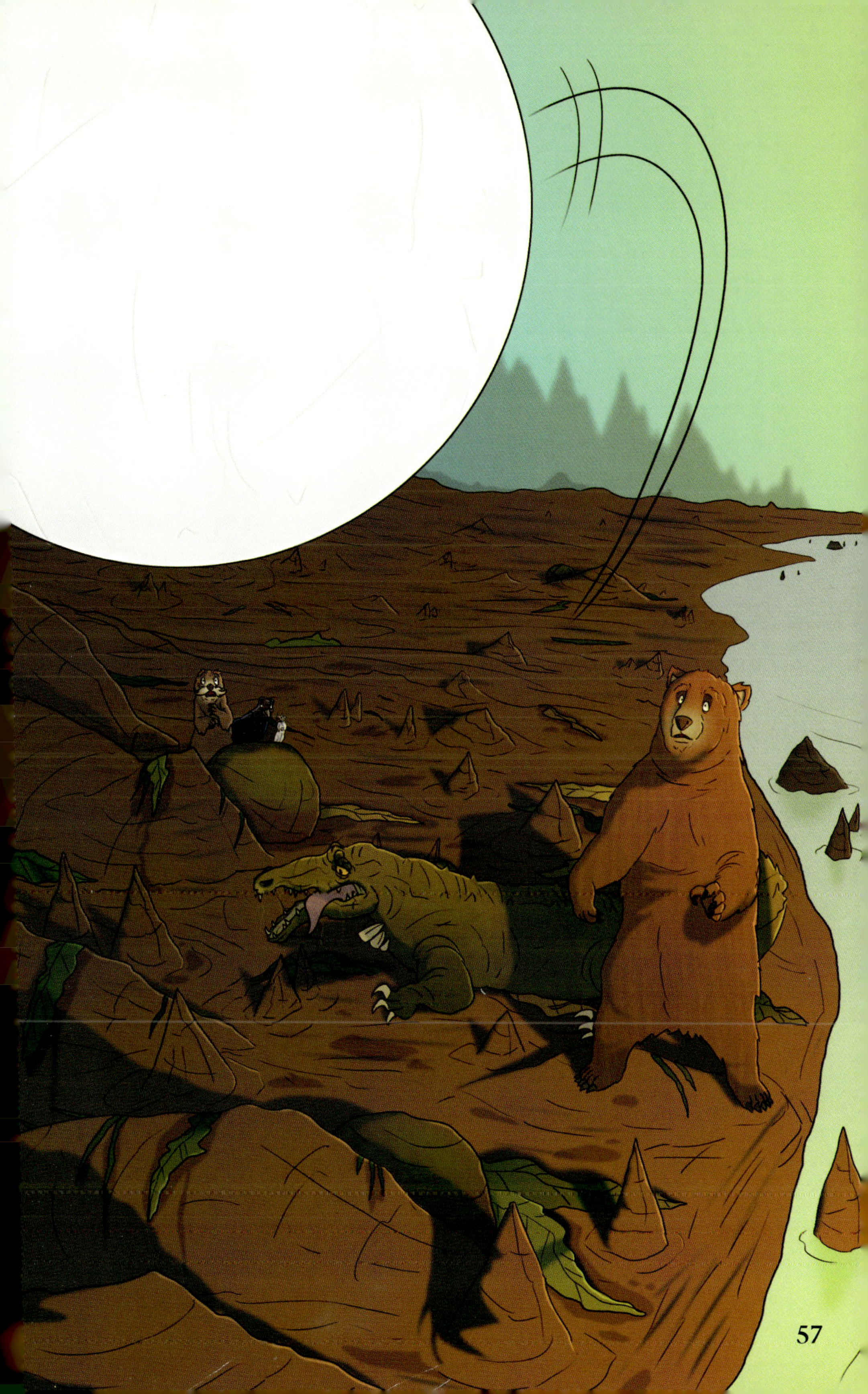

Chapter 7
Beautiful because of them

The pearl had gone. It launched from Crocodile's throat with a power and speed that made it nearly impossible to see. But Rat, Raven and Otter saw it fly straight up then vanish in the sky.

Much later, while the other animals wandered home, the three friends perched on the lip of the shell to watch the evening sky. They were hoping to find something that might be lost. They said little of anything, especially about how Crocodile and Bear left the shore without another word.

Raven was not angry with them, at least not at the moment, but she might be angry later on. The last few days had been so strange and exhausting that she did not know what to feel. She knew that Rat and Otter felt the same way.

Rat broke a long quiet spell to ask Otter how he knew about the way to remove the pearl from Crocodile's throat.

"I've got grandchildren, remember? You wouldn't believe the things they put in their mouths."

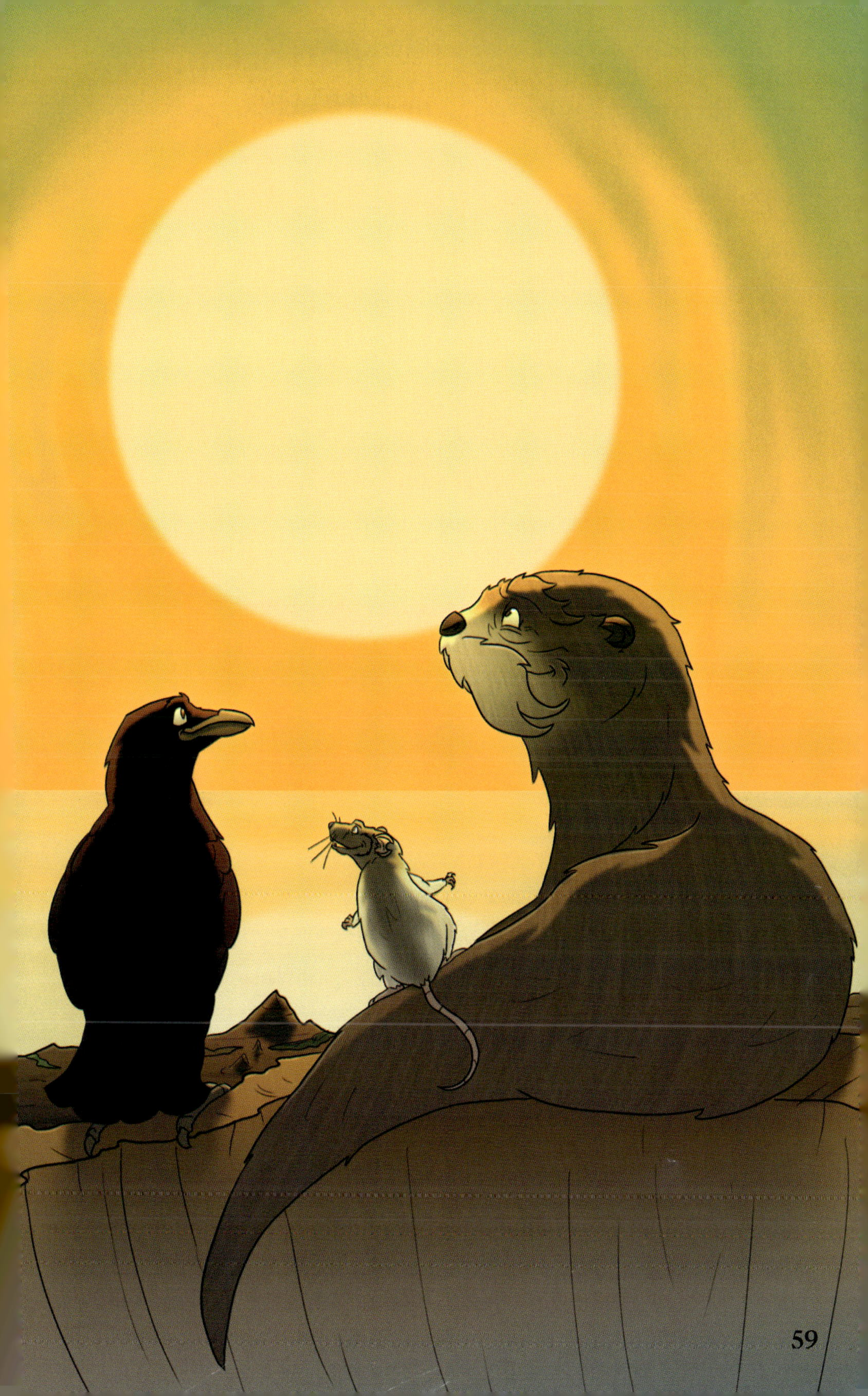

After the Sun went down, they rolled their heads back to stare at the bright new ball in the sky that lit up the darkness.

"Very pretty," whispered Otter. "It is very pretty, indeed."

Raven thought it was beautiful in spite of the dimples, pits and craters. Rat thought it was beautiful because of them.

Tracing his paw over one of the darker sections, Rat said, "There's a face."

Raven wanted to know whose.

"Nobody's. It's just a face."

She found a rabbit. Otter saw an octopus, or maybe a tree with a wide trunk. Rat spied two bear paws. Raven found a crab claw. When they ran out of things to see in the craters, they went back to admiring the whole thing.

Otter wondered, "How long before it'll come back down?"

Rat thought for a long time before saying, "Probably never. It shot out of Crocodile's throat so quickly that it's still moving. It's going a lot slower than when it started, and maybe too slow for us to notice, but it's still going. It'll stay up there, I think, moving a little bit."

Otter said, and Rat agreed, that it was nice the Sun had company.

This made Raven want to smile, but a beak and feathers are useless for that kind of thing, so she nodded instead.

"I think so, too. Everybody needs a friend."

The science behind the story

The Moon was once closer to Earth, but now it moves away. Because of how gravity works between Earth and the Moon, the Moon raises the water on Earth. These forces combine with others to drive the Moon away from Earth by nearly 4 centimetres a year. Scientists have worked out that as the Moon was formed 4.5 billion years ago, it has moved over 400,000 kilometres away from Earth.